Elsewhere

The Walt McDonald First-Book Series in Poetry

Robert A. Fink, *editor*

*Vanitas*, Jane McKinley
*Horse and Rider*, Melissa Range
*Leap*, Elizabeth Haukaas
*Wild Flight*, Christine Rhein
*The Clearing*, Philip White
*Burning Wyclif*, Thom Satterlee
*Slag*, Mark Sullivan
*Keeping My Name*, Catherine Tufariello
*Strange Pietà*, Gregory Fraser
*Skin*, April Lindner
*Setting the World in Order*, Rick Campbell
*Heartwood*, Miriam Vermilya
*Into a Thousand Mouths*, Janice Whittington
*A Desk in the Elephant House*, Cathryn Essinger
*Stalking Joy*, Margaret Benbow
*An Animal of the Sixth Day*, Laura Fargas
*Anna and the Steel Mill*, Deborah Burnham
*The Andrew Poems*, Shelly Wagner
*Between Towns*, Laurie Kutchins
*The Love That Ended Yesterday in Texas*, Cathy Smith Bowers

# Elsewhere

Poems

Kyoko Uchida

Introduction by Robert A. Fink

**Texas Tech University Press**

This book is typeset in Futura. The paper used in this book meets the minimum requirements of ANSI/NISO Z39.48-1992 (R1997). ∞

Designed by Kasey McBeath

Library of Congress Cataloging-in-Publication Data
Uchida, Kyoko.
Elsewhere : poems / Kyoko Uchida.
p. cm. – (Walt McDonald First-Book Series in Poetry)
"This twenty-first winner of the Walt McDonald First-Book Prize in Poetry unravels the landscapes of childhood migrations and passages across oceans and continents, seasons and languages, mapping the geographies of longing, loss, grief, and conflict"–Provided by publisher.
ISBN 978-0-89672-736-6 (hardcover : alk. paper)
I. Title.
PS3621.C45E47 2012
811'.6–dc23 2011051819

Printed in the United States of America
12 13 14 15 16 17 18 19 20 / 9 8 7 6 5 4 3 2 1

Texas Tech University Press
Box 41037 | Lubbock, Texas 79409-1037 USA
800.832.4042 | ttup@ttu.edu | www.ttupress.org

*For my parents,*
*who taught me*
*love of language and literature*

# Elsewhere

Poems

Kyoko Uchida

# Contents

# Acknowledgments

I am grateful to the editors of the following publications, in which some of these poems first appeared, a few in earlier versions:

*The Black Warrior Review*: "House"
*The Georgia Review*: "Dictionary," "After Weeks of Rain," "Inheritance"
*Grand Street*: "Needle," "Motion," "Peaches," "Taking Your Shoes Off"
*New Letters*: "Letter"
*Nimrod International Journal*: "Garden"
*The Northwest Review*: "Butter"
*Other Voices International Poetry*: "Against Images," "Elsewhere," "This Is Where," "Translation"
*Painted Bride Quarterly*: "Driving Lessons," "Compulsory Figures," "Snow-prints"
*Phoebe*: "Brother Tongue"
*Prairie Schooner*: "At Thirty"
*Quarterly West*: "Warranty"
*Runes, A Review of Poetry*: "Debt of Gratitude"
*Shenandoah*: "Indigo"
*The Virginia Quarterly Review*: "Curve," "Destination"
*Voices Israel Anthology*: "Crossing"

I would like to thank TTUP Poetry Editor Robert A. Fink, the Walt McDonald First-Book Competition in Poetry, and everyone who has helped make this book possible. I am especially grateful to my teachers Michael A. Kramer, James McMichael, the late A. R. Ammons, Phyllis Janowitz, Kenneth A. McClane, and Robert Morgan for their kind encouragement; Kimiko Hahn, for her summer 1999 class at the Asian American Writers' Workshop; fellow poets and writers Angela Shaw, Amy Sara Carroll, Nina Revoyr, and Amy Rowland for their friendship and faith; and my family, for their quiet support all these years.

# Elsewhere

Poems

Kyoko Uchida

I lost two cities, lovely ones. And vaster,
some realms I owned, two rivers, a continent.
Elizabeth Bishop, "One Art"

Maybe it's true that we are all from elsewhere or going elsewhere.
Kyoko Uchida, "Elsewhere" (personal essay)

In stories passed down to children, the hero quests in a straight line defined by courage and beauty and virtue, arriving at what we listeners require—success, blessing, happiness ever after. Who sets out to circle back, start over, or despair and stop? How many circuits to *elsewhere*? Isn't each departure the promise of *somewhere*—a home, family, the reward at the end of the line? What about the paradox of courting failure, knowing each orbit more familiar and strange, the addictive *elsewhere*? Maybe this time better? Maybe this time we won't circle "back to open wounds, tending ruins" ("Ruins")?

In her personal essay "Elsewhere" published in Cune Press's 1997 anthology *An Ear to the Ground: Presenting Writers from 2 Coasts,* Kyoko Uchida states, "Every place I've lived has been a temporary arrangement: I've always known that I'd leave. . . . I've come to inhabit a landscape of displacement—of arrivals and departures. I had already lost each place we lived years before I ever saw it." Paradoxically, each landscape she enters becomes "as familiar and as distant and inaccessible as the last. . . . This displacement is an intimate part of me, as well-known to me as my own body. It's the only constant I can claim."

Kyoko Uchida's poems in *Elsewhere* join beauty and intellect, with each section of the book thematically unified and coherent, an orchestration compelling me to participate, to approach again what it means to be me, to be human. As an editor, as a lover of fine poetry, I read expecting the poet to acknowledge my daily paradoxes, this life cycle, growth rings accumulating, my knowing of self. In *The Writing Life*, Annie Dillard says it this way: "Why are we reading if not in hope that the writer will magnify and dramatize our days, will illuminate and inspire us with wisdom, courage, and the possibility of meaningfulness?" Like Dillard, I read to recognize in the poet a fellow sojourner "set down here bewildered," engaged in our shared exploration of the "deepest mysteries." I don't expect, or desire, an answer. What I require is the experience, the poet's skilled depiction of our experience. Certainly a poem, a book of poems, should *be*, but shouldn't it also *mean*? *Elsewhere* is such a book, Kyoko Uchida such a poet.

Kyoko was born in Hiroshima, Japan, and spent her childhood in Hiroshima; Houston; Vancouver; Toronto; Orange County, California; and later Bordeaux, France. She earned a B.A. from the University of California at Irvine and an M.F.A. from Cornell University. She has lived in Washington, DC; Ithaca, New York; New York City; Jerusalem; and currently resides in Brooklyn. The structure of *Elsewhere* can be seen as a map of the poet's physical and emotional geography—a journey to elsewhere, but as we know, a map is never the journey, the quest. There is no push pin for Elsewhere.

The poems chart a sequence of beginnings and endings and beginnings and. . . . *Elsewhere* defines the poet as cartographer, each section of the book a map of place, geography, a literal backdrop for a metaphorical quest, not one plotted on a map but one interpreted through the "language of longing" ("In First Grade"), the "vocabulary of our hearts" ("Tangential"). This map takes us from Hiroshima, to California, to a road trip east across the United States, to New York, to Israel, to Brooklyn and to a recollection of places equally past and present (France, Houston, Arizona, New Mexico, Kansas), but *Elsewhere* is not a tourist's travel guide; it is a life, a cyclical route to *elsewhere*—that place in the heart, known and unknown, desired, compelling. Each poem seems an extended metaphor, layered thematic motifs circling throughout the book: a displaced persona paradoxically both seeking and rejecting the stability, the order of home, family, marriage—literal and symbolic places seemingly secure from the call to *elsewhere*, that place of gravity and also moving water—Heraclitus's river, each step a discovery, a possibly better self. It is a strange place requiring a new vocabulary to communicate what we desire even though we fear we don't. It is a place at war, mostly with ourselves.

*Elsewhere* begins and ends with weather, seasonal and almost always coming in fast as a storm ("Weather," "Drifts"), a life to be weathered. "At Thirty," the second poem in the book, explains how the Japanese view turning sixty as a celebration of "coming full circle, / returning our frail, shrinking bodies / to the ritual crimson clothes of a newborn." Endings are beginnings—"To know where a thing ends and another begins" ("To Know Where")—but no less painful for this knowledge. It is the living, the loving, in between that clarifies happiness, the possibility of joy "expected yet / miraculous every time" ("The Pursuit of Happiness").

Section One explores the meaning of the persona's place in her family, especially in relation to her mother "in mourning now, / for the daughter I am not, for the mother / I am not" ("At Thirty"). Communication is strained, "[t]hick-tongued" ("Inheritance"). In her "Japanese house," the persona thinks of herself as a "stranger," avoiding openings, "asking to be / locked out," "careful to see that the house is small" ("House"). And yet, she admits she fits "so easily again / into the childhood dimensions of this / Japanese house" ("House"). It is "a love story," a paradoxical love "so necessary that in the end / we must turn even our daughters out" ("Debt of Gratitude"). Growing up in Japan, the persona "learns early to live within / narrow limits," everything having its "assigned place, bound / by necessity, or beauty," contained by "the private rooms / of wordlessness, the boundaries within" ("Within").

Section Two plots the persona's cross-country trek from California to New York with a lover much older than the persona—"I have a weakness for / father figures" ("If I Refuse"). He is driving her to the East Coast and school. He will leave her and return to the opposite coast. She admits they have little in common. They measure silences. She desires their relationship "to be difficult, or / unlikely, or both"—"this being / wanted, wanting him" ("If I Refuse"). Her expectation is realized in the difficulties present in this *strange*, complex relationship, a vortex of warring emotions, absences lived in as a neighborhood ("Letter"), for years "traveling here in circles, / unknotting ourselves from each other" ("Motion"). She is "rehearsing for the next time," beginning again "shedding in slow installments what I've already / lost once" ("Beginning Again"). They have let each other go, and the persona can say her "sleep is dreamless, almost / easy," acknowledging the cycle of loss, that she has "been here /

from the beginning," that she "was only arriving / into the scene of your absence. / I've missed you already for years" ("Destination").

Section Three starts another cycle—marriage, beginning and ending, both feared and expected. The backdrop is Israel, mostly Jerusalem, with flashes of New York City and September 11, 2001, displacement and dissolution—"the torn pocket of my heart, where / everything fell through" ("Needle"). At first the persona and her husband construct a "most intimate grammar" *unspoken*, communicating through "shared laughter, dinners in, a touch, / like dancing to rain in the dark kitchen" ("I Should Tell You"), but the persona finds herself moving from room to room in the small hours of the night, an insomniac *vigilant* against herself, "against waking up alone" ("Insomnia"). After September 11, 2001, she knows her "geography has shifted to map what we are / without" ("This Is Where"). Hers is now an "abbreviated geography of pared-down needs" ("Cyclamens").

The cycle continues: "spring breaks out over Jerusalem / like a swift, fatal disease" ("Cyclamens"). The persona's thoughts turn more and more to her mother "orbiting, unbidden, your sadness / like some wayward moon" ("Missing"). The tensions between Israelis and Palestinians seem to reflect the unspecified rift in the persona's marriage leading to divorce: "we will settle / civilly what is left" ("Settlement"). It all seems anticipated, matter of fact—"as stingingly futile, as inevitable, as forgotten / as last year's war" ("Outside"). She acknowledges their pursuit of happiness was hindered by her husband's tending his "well-kept flowerbox," uprooting "anything faded or unsightly, / putting in what was already lovely, in blossom," while she "scratched at / hard red clay," tending "unruly mint and thyme, / misshapen squash," hoping these "indigenous, perennial, drought-resistant, / tough as weeds" herbs and vegetables "would nourish us" ("The Pursuit of Happiness").

The final section, Four, of *Elsewhere* locates the persona in Brooklyn, alone in a "fourth-floor walk-up . . . settling down to a quiet life indoors" ("Domestication"). Now the persona can declare, "I am domesticating my life. / I am learning to live in a small place" ("Domestication"). She thought she and her husband "were mapping the world / out of the wilderness we shared," but he was looking for "a sheltered clearing / deep in the forests of imported linens and furniture" arranged in "a lovely house of many rooms," while she preferred plotting "the purple clover field humming with light / or pebbles underwater sharp as broken glass / or the jeweled heat of sun-split figs" ("Domestication"). She acknowledges her ability "to inflict pain just by wanting, by wanting / something else" ("In First Grade"). Like music, the vocabulary of yearning goes beyond language ("Piano Lesson").

Friends who know her situation make her feel "as though made of glass: / not brittle but transparent, exposed, like / an X-ray emerging against artificial darkness" ("To Know Where"). She prefers being "a piece of green sea glass, worn round and smooth, / refracting light at funny angles" ("To Know Where"). She can now look back over her life to this point and see it as tangential, her need "to negotiate the space between *here* and / *there*," acknowledging she has ironically been traveling "the surest route to my mother's voice" ("Tangential"). She wishes to ask forgiveness of her mother "for misreading" their "trajectories, the time it takes to navigate / bodies of water and deserts unmentioned, / for still expecting her to ferry me across" ("Translation").

This final section being a kind of summing up, the persona's looking back on what has come before, especially her losses, enables her to recognize what she knew but didn't know, the paradox of the present being the past, "that we were already remembering / ourselves younger, in the foreground, / no longer there" ("Foreground"). Now she is "beginning to see the world without, / to *paint the shadows first*, though it's taken / twenty years" ("Corot, In The Evening"). She has *apprenticed* herself "to living alone" ("Corot, In The Evening"), more an acceptance than a resignation.

The final poem "Drifts" is appropriately paradoxical. The scene is the first snow storm of the season "dimming the traffic lights, erasing the sky," but the tone is peaceful, the snow canceling out "the stark silhouettes of branches and fire escapes / serrated against the white afternoon." "Snowlit," the "evening brightens," and the persona seems content to press herself "against the icy glass / as it blots itself out little by little." The evening continues to soften. The "hysteria of spinning tires" fades, as does the "clanging *scrape, scrape* against the sidewalk," as does the persona's "reflected double," disappearing "the way even one's own handwriting / becomes illegible in the failing light." Though a psychiatrist might claim otherwise, this concluding image does not seem a death wish, certainly not in the manner of Japanese suicides on the "sharp cliff off the Pacific known as / the Cape of Grief or of Writhing Feet," removing their shoes before exiting "onto nothing but air" ("Taking Your Shoes Off"). The persona's peaceful, even joyful, mood in "Drifts" seems parallel to that of the Japanese turning sixty, circling back to begin again as a newborn ("At Thirty"), wiser, though she will not know it yet.

Robert A. Fink
Abilene, Texas, 2012

# One

# Elsewhere

Poems

Kyoko Uchida

# Weather

The cherry blossoms come in
early this year, fast as a storm,
blinding and everywhere at once.
A rush of light thickens the veiled air
heavy with the quick hum of bees.
Already they dust these well-kept sidewalks,
snowing into our mouths and hair, relentlessly
white as bone, fine as ashes—
collecting beyond the hours of our watch
like foreign news overnight.
It is not enough to imagine
so many dead underfoot.
In the hush of a city buried ankle-deep,
we sleepwalk in spring colors as if
war were another season.

# At Thirty

At thirty my mother was seven months pregnant,
thin as milk and luminous in blues and ivories,
colors for grown, quiet women. She asks
what I am mourning in my terrible black clothes
at my age. Her daughter has grown into no one
she knows, and she is the one in mourning now,
for the daughter I am not, for the mother
I am not.

This year, turning thirty myself, the simplest math
surprises: my mother reaching twice that age.
At sixty we Japanese celebrate coming full circle,
returning our frail, shrinking bodies
to the ritual crimson clothes of a newborn.
For her birthday, someone else's daughter
would send a maroon sweater or a coral scarf,
but what I want to buy us both is
a red, red dress.

# Brother Tongue

In America
we were punished for speaking English
at home. Our parents didn't want us
to lose our mother tongue. We would
climb the peach and plum trees, fall
out of them, thighs cold and itching with
pee when we came to—I would
follow you onto the moon-
scape of fine-dusted anthills
cratered in your step. *Didn't know*, you'd say
in it, kneeling at the edge of the brown field,
unlacing my square-knotted sneakers to
slap away handfuls of ants biting
copper and soft. The other boys
knew better, chased the fat grasshoppers
and raced each other home. It is late, we are
five and a half and nine, you hold my ankle
in your small boy's hands as if to keep
the red welts from rising.
Of course,
we would learn to speak better English,
test where to put our feet and fast, a
fist sometimes, fickle words to fill our
mouths like teeth and figure out fitting in.
Even though the four-lettered ones were
yours to teach, we would come in like
foreigners together, and because we were
forbidden to, shared only in this
other, brother tongue.
We would learn again
not to speak at all. The place you've been
called back to had been yours first, too—

and you its only, firstborn, claim.
I write to you now in this tongue become
strange to us—I who have stayed, who
you say have strayed too far, who you
tell others will lie in telling myself
how you carried me the half mile back,
my shoes and arms swinging from your
sour neck, my naked feet burning bright in
your hands, pointing the way home, the way home.

# Inheritance

*August 6, 1995*

They begin to die early.
The first seedlings of basil and sweet marjoram
peel yellow, curl in the already parched light.
The fiftieth summer gathers, lengthens across
a heat wave, close and unforgiving as a wish.
The dill and parsley go, then the peas.
I am twenty-five and halfway there.
The sun, grown heavy, splits ringing and blunt,
crushes the black crown of my skull, the thin
weave of muscle at my neck.
My shoulders burn for the first time and
skin slips away from me, from the things
I try to hold: in the soft palms of hands, in
the hollow above my hip when I turn, there
is nothing. The slow length of each limb
comes into its own ache, leaden as if I've been
swimming. All day I taste salt on my lip.

This August I do not return to the city
where I was born, where they will gather
the evidence and read the lists of names.
News of Hiroshima washes against me
in waves that echo sea water beating.
Thick-tongued and without a center,
I squat down in the garden among the tall
fragrant weeds grown thick in place of harvest;
I count the new spots on my skin
that might signal cancer, what my mother
has taught me to watch for, my
inheritance turned inside out. In
the curve beneath my ribs where it is hidden,
they blossom like wildflowers in the crying heat.

# House

Perhaps if I didn't fit so easily again
into the childhood dimensions of this
Japanese house, the yellow kitchen light
and unswept staircase, I wouldn't be so much
a stranger here. Across the raised entry or

past low papered doorways, moss air loosens
pale to take me in. I avoid openings
the way I avoid the black tatami mat borders,
where I've been taught it is wrong to stand.
For in finding too soon again the worn patterns

of where I sit at the table or when I speak,
like our own laundry hung newspaper-grey;
in finding my place at the sink easy, I risk
the fine distances I've drawn myself against.
Nothing tells of absence here.

I move noisily, knocking into what has always
been there. In a house where walls are sliding
panels of wood and soft paper, I am asking to be
locked out. *I don't live here anymore.* That I am
not missed is irrelevant. In these rooms

without pictures of children, missing
is for the irresponsible, the ones who
do not return. Instead I sit like a spoiled
guest, listening for water in our speeches,
careful to see that the house is small.

# Butter

My mother couldn't make the sound of two t's, the quick
flutter of tongue against palate, hard stop: muttering
*but-ter, buller, budder* after me at ten, she drove me to
utter despair. Yet she'd studied Hemingway and Faulkner,
the Brontë sisters, Woolf; no other letter in the alphabet
made her stutter like this. She had little patience for such
unpretty sounds made for chattering by a mouth half-
shuttered against itself, putting its ends in-between.
So I cluttered my own daughter-tongue, scattered them
sharp as slow pitter-patter of water on rotting wood,
dull as the clatter of steak knives flashing against a
fine-patterned cloth. And later, hard as muscle,
soft as the tongue itself touching its wet tip
to the base of two teeth, almost then not, flirting
the way I never learned. Years later, much later,
the salt taste of someone else's on mine. Even then
what really mattered was how it flattered, the easy
trick of knowing how to say a thing like warmed
butter or something better, slick as *buttering him up.*
It had made my mother sick at school those
Occupation years, rich yellow squares of fat she wasn't
allowed to waste. It ran strong as hunger inside her
raw mouth, oiling the small working parts, loosening
the fettered tongue to say its animal smell
aloud. But it wouldn't fit, clotting thick in her throat,
and all of this going down rancid, bitter.

# Debt of Gratitude

They say it is a love story. I do not
deny it. She arrives in snow falling fast as any
longing, in white like a ghost or a bride.
In the folktale I remember, it is an old woman who
takes her in, whose husband once took pity on a crane.
Who else but a poor childless couple to be blessed
with a daughter and unending bolts of purest white silk,
rich as the moonlight she weaves by?

They say no, it is a young hunter instead, dumbstruck
and eligible, whose kindness she's come to repay.
At her loom each night she hides her feathered self
so that she might stay his wife, out of love. And it is
out of desire for her pale smooth neck that he breaks
his promise not to look. There is no other explanation.

In my version, by winter's end the old woman sees,
as only a mother would, that her daughter grows thin
with every thread. This is why she looks:
Every mother believes she has the right to know.
In the morning the crane must leave, weeping at the woman's
betrayal. It's as if all this time she'd been weaving
her own funeral shroud.

Or wedding dress. My mother says, *It's about time.*
Even in this children's tale of virtue and debt of gratitude,
a girl must weep for her husband, not her mother.
They tell me that I should have known all along.

They say it is a love story. I do not
deny it: a love so necessary that in the end
we must turn even our daughters out.

# Apology

It was an accident and it would never happen
again. In the slow, honeysuckle heat of Texas June
already thick with the drone of bees, we stood
side by side at the screen door, looking out at
the morning glories I'd planted for my first grade project.
While you'd been away, the vines had climbed quickly,
and now the buds wrapped tight as parasols were unfurling
white-streaked purples and cool, soft blues.
Light sharpened dizzying around them.
You'd leaned in, perhaps to point out a new bloom,
as any father might, when your lit cigarette grazed my arm.
I didn't mean to cry out, to twist away from your
startled touch. When I wouldn't let you see
but backed away toward my mother's voice,
you turned to stare out at the morning glories
and said, *It's alright. It doesn't hurt.*
And I wanted so much to believe you.

# Within

Growing up in three-room high-rise apart-
ments and miniature houses crowding
small islands, one learns early to live within
narrow limits, and even those bound-
aries are permeable, the walls of rooms
rice-papered partitions slid open, closed,

without a sound. They let in shadows close
up, shut out little, merely set apart
space temporarily—not so much rooms
defined as according to the crowd and
the hour, what each needs to be, each bound
to change with the light slanting within.

Thus, what is the den to start with, in
turn, might become the parlor, the guests closed
off from the household. When the children bound
home, it might be the dining room, a part
of the kitchen now, warm dishes crowding
the knee-high table. Perhaps then the room's

cleared, the cushions stacked away to make room
to unfold the bedding hidden within
paneled shelves, where things are kept from crowding
the tatami floor. Living in such close
quarters, we learn to make ourselves a part
of the arrangement, of what we're each bound

to. Everything has its assigned place, bound
by necessity, or beauty. No room
for clutter—as if one owned space apart
from others. We must rearrange within
our small, precise belongings, hold them close;
to keep our separate selves from crowding

others, must discern the needs of the crowd in
advance, without overstepping the bounds
of subtlety: bring tea, draw a bath, close
the door. Nothing goes unnoticed—cold rooms,
objects displaced—the order we live with. In
the dark kitchen, a woman sits apart.

Crowding out our own need to live apart,
we close in on even the private rooms
of wordlessness, the boundaries within.

# Compulsory Figures

I want to ask you: In those classrooms still
new to you, do they sit waiting, their hands
folded clean, like rows of
faceless daughters? In my dream
my nails are trimmed and I hold the pen
correctly. There are hundreds of us, all
anxious for equations, answers to questions
we do not know to ask.

I want to ask you: Do you give them
what you've refused me these
open-handed years, slow
compulsory figures to begin with,
simple formulas to work? Or is there
among them the daughter you've
always wanted, the one who speaks clearly,
unafraid, who knows to grow up
on her own? Without surprise, without
expectations, how could I have
impressed you, where could I
finally stop? In my dream you
never arrive. I will be there, always in
the back, long after the room goes
empty. For you are
in my teachers' distances, in their
forgetting my name.

# The Good Woman

He speaks of you to those who love him,
knowing that they do, that they will betray
no one. Me, for example. One by one, he unwraps
the kitchen details and fine bone clutter, as if
to leave them with me for safekeeping.
Perhaps it is the only tenderness he knows:
how you run barefoot after the children
wet from their bath, insist on French pastries,
refuse to be practical.
*Stubborn as a child*, he says, but he knows
I'll take your side in everything, always
the good woman who knows her place.
He trusts me as he trusts you not to ask
why he is late, though ashamed only of how
helpless he is before your moods and dutiful lunches,
your untended household faith.
Afraid you wouldn't care, he orders another glass
to talk of you, whose name I do not know.
He asks nothing but patience. It is
all I have, knowing that he'll look for you
first in the children's room, where you've fallen asleep
reading to them, so he can take your glasses off,
careful not to wake you, not to let them break.

# April

April I find myself on the same blue
maps of eucalyptus, of routines and weather
returns, only a little less sharp than the year
before. On foreign water I sit
with my feet over a row of painted boats
and think of what crimes I must be guilty.
The walls here are white and uneven,
the sidewalk centuries old. These
are the hours of glass, of
falling grains of sand.
I am filtering this brittle aching
from the specific absences, making it
a more willing part of myself, part
of the pulse of seasons.
It is something we walk with,
carry with us, careful as if it were
a rare seashell, a jewel, a lover;
it sits next to us when we eat, lies
cold against our chests in bed.

# Two

# Elsewhere

Poems

Kyoko Uchida

# If I Refuse

If I refuse to touch him
in public but sleep with my fingers
wrapped around his thumb at my
mouth, it is because I have a weakness for
father figures and like to think how much
older he is than I, and to remind him, too.

There is a perverse satisfaction in
seeing how little we have in common,
in measuring our silences; as if
the strangeness of our meeting here
could give it meaning, make it
less a choice and more honest.
Only this distance to bridge can keep us
together, keep us from seeing that there is
no good reason. His knuckles ridge
heavy-boned, creased, where I try to
read them with my palm.

I want this to be difficult, or
unlikely, or both; to know that it runs
against judgment. For otherwise,
it comes far too easily, this being
wanted, wanting him.

# Abundance

Earthquake weather, we'd say later on,
but that end of June, I wouldn't know
the difference in heat, just desert ridges
turning in grades of red. Though hidden
from the road, the clustered rocks give
no shelter in the arrowed sun, where we
wash in cotton underwear and shades.
You scrub my back with both hands.

Everything is thick and pressing:
Joshua trees stiff with insect sounds; the air
hung closed, then moving in heavy sheets,
blunt against my stomach; the hard
dust. The plain purple flowers I crush
walking. Lizards come out, glitty as tin.
Left out all morning, spare, the water
bows my body down in hot, uneven spurts,

stinging almost mineral. I can smell it
lifting, like the weak castile soap's
peppermint in my throat, like the fine
points of sweat already rising to your skin.
And it is the angle of leaning
my head into your hands, to be washed,
sunlit like that, fingers running tight
the length of hair, that I'd remember

first, in mid-winter, at a bath
on the Seto Inland Sea. Beyond glass
islands flatten, gathering dark as the roots of
my hair. Backs of knees; ankles; a rib; under

so much water, where nothing touches me:
edges fill, move away in rings. I am
weaving into water each need that I have
names for, learning again the parts of my body.

# Driving Lessons

1.
Following August across New Mexico borders
into rain so fast grinding glass and asphalt,
I lose the white markings where the lanes go,
numbers on road signs, arrows. I can't see
the other cars or hear them. I'm negotiating
windshield wipers, still learning to shift;
weaving stupidly through Gallup, missing
interchanges, overpasses, merging or gone.
On impulse I'd stop anywhere, this itinerary
for leaving: inches-thick sheets of water
sweep sideways, edges running together like
paint, until the car merely drifts in some
general direction: There. East. Forward.
My knuckles pale, a dull itch where
my arm has gone numb. He says, *Try to stay*
*on the road. Watch where the pavement ends.*

2.
Later, the terrain emerges
vertical and edged. Cliff sides wall in
broken shades of rust and flushed
magenta, ribboned stark for miles. He says,
*Here. Look on your left. I'll hold the wheel.*
Instead I turn to watch his face: the low
sunk slope of cheekbone; the vein-traveled
throat; eyes steady grey on the road.
A loose fist has the steering wheel
near the bottom, keeps it in place,
his shoulder leaning in a little, toward me.
*Left,* he says. *Look to your left.*

3.

The mistake is in learning the clutch on
his car, packed with my belongings, everything
I am taking with me, and him.
The car runs difficult under the weight,
slow climbing even the slighter grades,
the two-lane highway near Kansas.
Through dust-blown towns where it turns
Main Street or Central, I avoid stop signs and
lights; I have trouble stopping then
gearing into first, never know
how much to give, or where it catches.

The next time I'm in third with too much
distance on a late yellow light, I run it,
his voice sharp against the windshield where
I see it turn red. Someone honks,
but I can't stop here and stall again,
not now, I have to get on with it, this
driving myself away from where he lives.
It shouldn't be that difficult or slow.
Past the town's end, I'm speeding now too,
tears dripping like rocks into my lap, and
ignoring for the next mile his voice,
weary, yielding: *Pull over. I'll drive.*

# Warranty

At breakfast after you headed
back to California, I cut my left
index finger with the bread knife
you'd bought me, a housewarming gift
(and the skillet and screwdriver set)
I wouldn't buy myself, asking
what was wrong with the ones I had.
It'd be safer, you'd argued,
designed to cut bread; besides,
it came with a warranty.

There is a word for this
taking charge of my needs, of my
new apartment where you cannot stay,
furnishing it with your absence.
You mean only to see that I am
safe, that I lack nothing. Yes.
This is your defense against my
leaving, coming here; is a way of
accounting for, of making this room
yours, so you could tell it again,
what goes in it.

In the meantime, I cut myself open,
distracted, wishing myself strange.
Clean as an eyelid, the wound gapes on
bloodless, unblinking, my knuckle
gone whiter than bone. Imagine
deserts, reefs of pink coral, cactus fields
or anemone; how foreign landscapes
flower under skin, careless of their jeweled

mouths. Warranties expire. Now
I grow impatient with healing, with pale
cleft cells waiting blind for unnamed seasons,
not yet in full blossom with news of you.

# Letter

I buy houseplants to distract myself,
fuss over the ink-black touch of soil, worry
about water, about sunlight. You are
somewhere between Seattle and San Francisco
and I am learning to resist
making each day a white
waiting room, each hour a door
I enter and exit.
The task is like that of rearranging these rooms:
I hang pictures, stack my books,
move a chair up to the open window,
washed full of new branches, rooftops,
a fire escape. I might finger its peeling iron
and think, *I'll climb out there and read*, or
guess at the angle its shadow would be cast in
come February, on a rare sunny morning.
I have moved into your absence, this new
address, with my books and winter clothes;
I am learning to live here.
I am getting to know the neighborhood.

# Snowprints

Gravity, too, grows thick with snow,
accumulates inch by inch,
but the sensation is of flying.

I am moving over white space as it
takes itself up, the storm lifting east and
fast about my ankles, in my pockets
where my hands are tucked with change.
I'm running out of milk, out of time
in open snowlit streets; and retracing
two blocks home from the store,
I can't find my own footprints
anymore. Not erased but
filled in, the way absences fill.
It takes no time, as if snow
fell more quickly there.
Where all winter I saw nothing, branches
brighten like stitches of lace.
Something had been there: leaves, or
the yellow clutch of bird feet, balloons.
In the crease of my coat, the pressure of
hands, an embrace. We leave no evidence.
I could lose my way easily, the path
no longer familiar, untraveled,
stranger for having been here before.
We answer the same distances, each time the first.

# Indigo

What I see now in our snapshots
together is the hole in your T-shirt,
a torn seam at your left shoulder, dark
in the sun. Already up close, you can see
the indigo thread coming out, and this is
what worries me, how fast a thing
unravels. From the loose weave of what
covers us, touches our freckled skin, we are
open to desire or absence.
We count on the way our clothes keep us
together, separate and intact,
though we know better. We are
no closer beneath the careful fabric,
the small, easy buttons—only more
honest, unyielding, foreign. Nor are we
any safer, any more beyond touch
across heavy cotton, a white linen sleeve.
And if the distance we've sewn together
is thin, what begins to give
has been there all along: always
how things come apart into their own
basic pieces, all texture and hue of color,
all fiber and cut and bone, where
we are most ourselves revealed.
This time I want to take each unbroken
thread between my fingers, worrying it,
undoing slowly what I know to follow
where it takes me, how it ends.

## Curve

Nothing had warned me of this
follow of a line, the honeyed
reach forward of a shoulder, rib,
a body arriving into the mirror.
I'd never had curves before, just
the fickle, straight figure of an
almost-child, all stops and edges,
elbows, tinny bones like false starts:
next to you, it's become something
else, more my own, untold.
I am learning to see myself
sweeping, sinuous, coming into
the shape your desire takes.

—Is it enough?
What you've come to want of me,
want me to be now occupies, renames
my stolen body. Those warm and
well-known curvatures are not mine.
I grow heavy with your
aging wish, the pale and sunny hours
of your future, so kept and solitary,
so wrought with love it makes you
helpless. You've waited so long
already. My belly swells
luminous with its false, only absence,
swims with a promise never
answered, hard as bone.
It is beautiful as they say, all
milk and translucent where it kicks.

For now it is perfect, this roundness
between us: no more small silences run
sharp from use, no need to press ourselves
torn into angles, negotiating space
where we do not meet. When we lie
side to side, we fit closely, without effort;
we are no longer careful with each
other, our separate bodies, as we wait
for the break already beyond us.
The distance we touch across grows
full, circular, unspeakably rich.

# Motion

You are surprised at how easy it is, this
breaking away as you must think of it, nearly sorry for being
in motion so soon past our own departures, our ends.
Perhaps you'd imagined a heart's
old gravity, its wound ribbon white, unraveling
only at the speed of grief: small turnings
evenly arcing. You forget that bodies in motion tend to
stay in motion, repeat themselves like the fine, patient
weave of lace until they lose themselves. For years
together we'd been traveling here in circles,
unknotting ourselves from each other.
We'd been gaining momentum the way we'd gathered
place names on maps, long hours of highway or of
wine or getting dressed, matchbooks, used books, recipes,
lies, and each other's hair in our fists as we slept.
Even the earliest slow morning loops back, spirals
away from a center, opening and opening again its pale-
butter light, fast toward the next time we touch or cannot;
for we must always leave ourselves behind.
Now you find yourself arriving where you'd been
headed all these years, the new white lace, the ribbons
gathered thick and spinning in your open hands, and
at the end of it, someone else.

## From Between Us

It is not change we fear in each other, but the absence
of change in ourselves, hard evidence of having lived
nothing beyond the expected, not enough
to show in our bodies, our easy gestures.
Anything would do: the way you hold a coffee cup
or the timing of my breath when I say how
busy I've been with things that go unnamed. We recall
useless details to close up like fossils, to fix as
far away as possible from the present us.
I want you to tell me I am different.
It's been only a few years and haven't we
always been friends? It is across brittle air, full
of our woundedness and equal withdrawal,
that we know each other now, sense that if we've
won no ribbons, there are without fail the
unseen brutalities, braved, still healing, and in
far deeper places than we would allow.

# What Comes Next

*for Connie*

February runs end-stopped,
inevitable as what you knew
to be wrong with this place,
as the way things spiraled beyond you.
Seventh Avenue brightens with the season's
last snow. This time a year ago I didn't know
where you were headed, the only one, it seems.
Geography was no excuse, for I'd misread
distance from the beginning.
On this other coast it seems almost possible to go on
pretending you're still in transit, as if I could exchange
your absence here for your presence there,
waiting for you to arrive into the heavy sunlight
everywhere in the only pictures I have of you.
Crossing Macdougal with you, visiting that last September,
I'd thought only of how far you'd traveled, of
what maps we'd unravel between us; I couldn't see
you'd already begun to leave. What comes next
does so without itinerary or destination,
and this year only spring approaches.

# Ruins

From the beginning it was ruins
we visited, what weathered and open
remains of others passing or coming together
like this, or just things, either left
or abandoned. I held the map on my knees, always
the one to get us lost.

Then again, we'd begun with what we'd lost
already: luggage, accents, fights, what ruins
a certain year in college, your voice, fathers always
absent. We'd unbuttoned our shirts and laid open
the smooth scar tissue of what was left
to heal over, of what we'd worked to hold together.

This is the way we were together,
traveling down roads I'd been lost
on with other boys to bars where you'd left
with other women. It was the ruins
of our bodies that we loved in each other: the open
wreckage of broken bone and skin, always

torn in places never imagined but familiar, always
returning to what could not be recovered in charting together
sites of accidents, battles, even losing our way on the open
highway. I was distracted by rearview mirrors; you lost
your temper each time I missed an exit, a turning, ruined
our careful itinerary saying *right* instead of *left*.

In Santa Fe, it began to snow our last evening as we left
the emptied museum, late as always
for dinner and each quietly sifting the ruins
of our bruising hours together.
It came down so fast, hard as pebbles or corn, we lost
track listening to them fall intact against the glass. *Open*

*the window*, you said. Outside the only diner still open,
we chased each other drunk and ankle-deep in snow, left
footprints zigzagging empty streets, until lost
again, we found ourselves retracing them, always
our own passages out. Alone or together
we traveled only to the same unsecret ruins.

What is left tells only of what's been lost,
is always redundant. This is how we were together,
circling back to open wounds, tending ruins.

# Destination

In my dream summers before, you are the one
leaving. After the long-rehearsed
precise movements of my departure, I'd
misunderstood: the pale green ticket in my hand,
one way, not for sale. I've come
too early to the vast and mirrored station, where
you, already there, point to blank faces of
clocks scrubbed clean of numbers, telling
hands. You say, *Six-thirty*, your voice
run soft with small impatience, the way
you'd told me earlier that year how your
second wife had left, leaving only her
name out. This is where a paper-blue shadow
lifts across the floor from your feet, cut
predictably woman-shaped, thin as airmail
and faceless beneath a wide-brimmed hat
from summer films. The doors shut
slow motion on you two, though I hold
the ticket. They should; this is where it ends.

For weeks before I moved here, where I'd
write from, where you'd call, I dreamed only
of your leaving. I had it like night fever.
I recognize the woman now, by her nervous walk
in mirrors. After so much travel, long wintering
in the sealed touch of envelopes, we've let
each other go; my sleep is dreamless, almost
easy. There's no train, for I've been here
from the beginning: I was only arriving
into the scene of your absence.
I've missed you already for years.

# Peaches

Afterwards, you fed me peaches
cut into cold quarter moons and
tart, not yet ripe. You were late
for my appointment because you'd
stopped for them on the way, three
small peaches, the first of the season.
Later you wondered why I was
bruised like bad fruit, my arms
raw, stained wine and violet where
the needles had gone in, hip bone and thigh
where they had not. You who loved
the story of the boy who leapt in full armor
out of a peach, came floating down the stream
to an old woman washing clothes.
(The Japanese were always finding children
in peaches and bamboo, but they all left,
crossing the ocean or riding to the moon.)

You peeled quick crescents and fed me
by hand, the sharp scent of what is
not yet there. I opened my mouth
in penance. You'd chosen them for me,
touched each one in its turn, weighed them
against your wrist, considered their
blush and curve. In your palm they'd
smelled easy, warm as a kept promise.
You'd held them as you'd held me,
swollen, each one a late moon turned
sour, too early to tell; as you would later,
when I'd grown thin from staring.
Now you cut them open one by one,

with a knife, out of love.
But only blood appears, and the hard,
bitter pit of it in my mouth,
which you are careful to remove.

# Beginning Again

You want to get past it, want me
to be whole again, to return to where
we were. We accuse each other
of cutting our losses. You, too, have paid in
waiting-room hours, long-distance muteness
by the minute. I do not count the change
but the long unbrokenness of months in a year
against shades of red, salt scent of knives or of
belladonna; for it is difficult to remember what
I haven't yet lost when I must begin again each time,
shedding in slow installments what I've already
lost once, rehearsing for the next time.
This is what we call healing.
In the meantime I listen for the steady song of car alarms
while snow pulses *penance, penance.*

# February

Each winter she comes to me naked
in black and white, mottled and
eyeless as the moon.
This February I count again
the twenty-eight days I counted then, and past.
In the garden the perennials need trimming
before the thaw, before new growth can begin.
But this year spring arrives early, the sun
leaning heavily against the faded fence. Already
the dark-headed crocuses and irises are out,
their knife-edged green insistent, everywhere.
I take my shears to the gnarled miniature roses,
Russian sage, lavender, rue. For what buds
too soon on a rare warm day,
what is cut back too late, will be lost
to the last freeze and won't come in
again in time to bloom.
For this is what I let go:
all the seasons I will never have.

# Elsewhere

It does not come easily.
It takes years of learning to see ourselves
abandoned. The city is more April at night
than during the pale yellow day,
the dogwood blossoms luminous as
the false light of snow. All evening
the news flickers blue across the street.
And whose grief will I dream of tonight, here in
the borrowed safety of my well-rehearsed fears?
Our sidewalks are mined with tulips
blood red or bubble gum, bruised purple.
We are not safe from ourselves, our
unflagging forgetfulness in the face of
children laughing, of our separate hungers,
what we call our lives.

Elsewhere another war begins.

# Elsewhere

Poems

Kyoko Uchida

# Three

# Elsewhere

Poems

Kyoko Uchida

# Needle

I dreamed of swallowing a quick-
silver needle, cold as the mirror I stood in,
pinning heavy white folds of a dress to skin
naked as a hooked fish, sewing myself
in. Small double stitches to hold together
these wrists and knees loose as change,
to tailor each line, this breath to the next,
threading myself one eye at a time.
I needed alterations at the hem and waistlines,
the untidy mouth. I swallowed the needle then,
wriggling out of my own careful seams, my skin
catching. It pierced my tongue, went down
sharp as someone else's breastbone on its way
to the torn pocket of my heart, where
everything fell through.

# Garden

In the ruined garden it is my mother
I grieve for, her attempt year after year
to keep order, to keep up appearances. I spent
wet green summers weeding our narrow yard
after breakfast, before the noon heat struck, while
my mother hung out the wash, out of sight.
Squatting among her morning glories and nasturtium,
I pulled up what had sprouted overnight, their roots
fragrant with evening rain. I gathered in my hands
what was unwanted and wild, learning to distinguish
what to love, to discard. Working on my knees
around the carefully arranged boulders growing
soft, dark moss would teach me discipline,
to know what endures. Yet by mid-August
I couldn't keep up with the daily crop of weeds,
and my mother gave in each summer
in silence. Now in my own garden
nothing I plant takes hold, only this
unasked-for bounty of weeds. Each evening
I take in this bitter harvest, this weeding out of
what is too unruly in me, this knowing that
it will be there again tomorrow, regardless.

# I Should Tell You

That the Japanese word for *I love you*—
so embroidered, operatic, it shames
the nakedly fine distinctions it names—
is spoken only in films or by *gaijin* who

mispronounce it *I should tell you*, undo-
ing our most intimate grammar made strange
by the saying, blunt as staking claims.
Perhaps I *should* tell you but shouldn't have to:

My hand in yours in your coat pocket holds
the impossible in any language.
Not presuming but learning to listen,
to trust ourselves to the unspoken told
in our shared laughter, dinners in, a touch,
like dancing to rain in the dark kitchen.

# Against Images

Against images repeated everywhere of
ash and slow-motion falling
of bodies, steel, glass and silence
against the heavy roar of helicopters,
the sirens' numbing chorus—against all this
the tomato blossoms open
late, lit yellow as tiny flames
without hope of fruit.
Untended, the sidewalk garden goes wild,
the zinnias' fraudulent red too rich,
the sage grown thick as fur.
Still we hold on to the images,
say that debris *rained down,*
that bits of paper *fell like snow*
even across the water in Brooklyn.
We know that there is no comfort in this,
that the seasons change without us.
But we have no language for what we have seen—
not yet—and must make do with
what is left to us.

# Insomnia

Sometimes love resembles
exhaustion in its sheer brightness,
a blinding white sheet over my head
like a shroud, covering my eyes
against sleep. The space our bodies cut
between us intrudes, seeps through my bones
porous with want, fevered and weightless.
I move from room to room with a heavy book,
turning on all the lights. I tend nightly
to this brittle harvest of hot, dusty bulbs,
the small hours bleached of your touch
as vigilance against myself,
against waking up alone.

# This Is Where

This is where it happened.
Where I'd once worked across the street from
the towers where that day my friends made it
down forty-four flights of emergency stairs.
Where I'd once gone lunchtime-window-shopping or
to get passport photos at the same booth where
one friend had dropped off her film
from my wedding the week before.

A platform has been built from which to view
what is gone. From here
everything looks unfamiliar:
the hotel, the department store, the church
all unrecognizable at this new angle, as if
geography has shifted to map what we are
without: not the absence of what was
here, but an alien terrain unimagined.
When the wedding pictures believed lost turned up,
still undelivered that morning, they, too,
had become strange, unrecoverable,
our own faces no longer knowable,
only our dresses intact.

# Pomegranate

You teach me to eat pomegranates, jewel-toned seeds
as bright and hard as promises.
You pry each one from its intricate chamber,
careful not to break it between your fingers,
not to let it run. It is a delicate operation, this
feeding of our childhoods to each other, our
separate memories unearthed after years together.
I'd imagined something thick and pulpy,
smelling of blood or sex or both, but this is
a different kind of richness, light-filled, precise:
each seed shaped like a drop of wine,
staining everything it touches with its
tart, airy scent of abundance.
No wonder Persephone took them from the stranger's hand,
the seeds' ruby brilliance reminding her of warmth,
of all she missed and would, as a result,
lose again and again.

# Crossing

At Qalandia we cross back on foot:
a mud-deep path between concrete barriers,
shadowed by the wall, graffiti of twisted steel and rubble,
barbed wire tangled to illegible script.

The few men shuffle single-file, unspeaking,
their hands and faces emptied.
The women overflow their waiting area, a mass of hip bones and elbows
pressed against one another, fingers clasping bundles, briefcases,
small clammy hands, so many tongues clucking, shushing, sighing.

The light turns green; we surge against the cage-like turnstile,
two or three women squeezing into each quarter-turn, calling
for their daughters to stay close. When an arm or bundle is
caught in the bars, the others impatiently push it through.
We cannot see the soldiers; only the word *visa* comes across.
Now and then the turnstile reverses direction, pushes someone
back into the crowd, where she gropes her way out
as though blinded. We others wait.

Again we cling to the rotating grate, the metal bars
cold in spite of all the palms.
Among many hands I press my passport to the grimy glass.
Another green light, another turnstile, and
I stumble into open space, blinking,
as though I have crossed some distance:
not far, just to a place where my body has been neatly
segmented, then reassembled on the other side, but
in the wrong sequence—so that a tiny muscle
keeps clenching and unclenching itself, involuntarily.

## Keepsake

Why you keep returning I do not understand.
I have not forgotten you or neglected your claim.
Nor do I regret you, your absence
as necessary as salt, as blood, for me to be
here, as essential as my own fisted muscle.
Yet even here you keep me company,
in the white hum of stones, in the false snow of
almond blossoms, in the hills' olive haze, or
fattening and fading with the hot Eastern moon.
You need not worry, no one will take
your place. I have kept you as I might keep
a promise, a secret, a diary in a language I cannot read,
a bleak faith, or time.
Meanwhile, there is nothing you could want here:
only the laundry hanging stiff on the line,
white shirts blinding in the dust-bleached sun.
And the desert years stretching as far as the Dead Sea.

# Cyclamens

It is always April in Jerusalem.
When the rain lifts,
all along the gutters and chalk-dust ravines
bloom knots of pastel-colored plastic bags and bottles,
blowing among the ubiquitous cyclamens.
A fevered profusion of mouths pink as wounds:
every courtyard and alleyway overrun by sickly kittens
that the neighbors feed and do not neuter, they say,
*out of pity. They, too, want to live.*
At the open window:
the sharp note of geraniums, cat piss,
arguments in Russian, a halting violin,
dishes breaking and the damp hush afterwards,
each detail ordinary, needless,
like spring in any city.

Across the park's freshly mown grass,
schoolboys flock, white shirttails flying, to ask
the time, only that's not what they want to know—
what they've been taught not to ask their own.
For them, too, each new season
is punishment.
At the far end of the Jaffa Road,
some days the uniforms are olive green, others blue.
One comes running, eager and freckled, to ask for my passport
but merely thumbs it, disappointed.

Today, too, they are kicking over the cardboard boxes
of vendors without permits, or favor; bundles of
*zataar*, grape leaves, socks and cell phone cases
tumble into the trash-strewn rocks below Damascus Gate.
Only the children's darting shadows, the grandmothers' murmurs,
the hue of the late splintered light remain.

I have learned my way here and back,
the shortcuts down steep stairways, the better market stalls,
the bench by the monastery:
my abbreviated geography of pared-down needs.
In a few weeks there will be green almonds and mulberries,
later yellow figs, then evening-dark ones,
then peaches fragrant as fire.
The women will not let me touch the fruit.

And again spring breaks out over Jerusalem
like a swift, fatal disease.

# Missing

You are not dead.
Nor are you absent, any more than I am
to myself in sleep, nor any more distant than
the span of continents darkened between us,
oceans unspoken in our inverted geographies of night.
I move from coast to coast, lake effect country to
island and desert cities—the point of reference ever
constant so there is no East, West, Middle East, or out—
trying to locate my gravity beyond you,
but only spinning through time zones
all in present tense.

It is only for what I am not that I miss you: a mother.
For you are in everything else that I do.
Because you taught me to sing the alphabet,
to fight, to keep silent, to say no, to become—
I can never become you.
And because you never asked me to,
in my false daughter's logic I have already failed:
I can only be that which you are not.
What separates us is what keeps me yours,
orbiting, unbidden, your sadness
like some wayward moon.

# Unlikelihood

Take nothing for granted, not even
gravity, or a job at half-minimum wage.
Nothing is guaranteed: Tomorrow
you may not get to work, even only
to be told that you will not be paid.
Your bus may be stopped; you may be ordered
off, to lift up your shirt in the asphalt sun
to show that you are naked under your clothes.
If you should make it back, you may find your house
demolished, your wife and children sifting through rubble,
dust rising fine as salt, white as bone—
but only if your children come home from school.
A wall may sprout across your olive groves,
blooming concertina wire, your father on the other side
unable to reach the hospital.
This is your life.
The unlikelihood of such a life is undisputed.
In fact, it is simply unimaginable. Instead, they say:
Just think how much you have to be thankful for
every day that an apple falls from a tree,
instead of other objects that might fall out of the sky:
a homemade rocket, artillery shells, a guided missile,
a suicide bomber's severed head,
ashes from a crematorium.

Instead, we say nothing:

# Settlement

The landscape I have left
shifts constantly beyond
my sightline: I follow
the distant seasons: dust,
rain, cyclamens, desert,
tear gas, harvest, settle-

ment; sorting what settles
in this soil, what is left
on the surface: desert
salt, grit, air parched beyond
breathing, bitterest dust,
with nothing to follow

but absence. The follow-
ing facts are now settled
between us, like fine dust:
The terrain we have left
to cross stretches beyond
the Dead Sea, the desert;

we neither deserted
the other nor followed
far enough but beyond
ourselves; we will settle
civilly what is left.
Under skies blown to dust

we each retreat to dust
off our lives in deserts
not our own, neither left
nor right, no map to follow,
no land to settle,
only to move beyond.

We cede all else beyond
memory but the dust-
green olive trees settled
deep into deserted
streets, where voices follow
those who have never left.

Left beyond to follow:
desert dust to settle.

# Outside

But outside, beyond the kitchen window,
the almond blossoms startled us each winter
even though we were careful to watch for early signs,
tried to anticipate the tightly wound buds
unfurling overnight, all at once—
a miniature blizzard of luminous white,
a spectacle as extravagant as a wedding dress
thrown off, as unsettling as a fever flaring up after quiet,
as stingingly futile, as inevitable, as forgotten
as last year's war.

# Regret

I regret only
the jar of chestnut honey
we'd brought back from four days in Italy,
how we'd hoarded it—
measuring out precious drizzles for company:
the heavy scent of hot, sleepy villages,
horse-dotted pastures, orchards swimming with
the thick, grainy glow of late fig season,
the morning climb up the wooded goat trail
to the shadeless ridge, the bleating deafening
over the herder's boom box.
Perhaps at the time it had seemed
too luxurious, too deeply golden and warm,
as if we'd known we had to make it last.
I confess I would have taken it if I could,
smuggled it out in my boxes of books or clothes,
but I admit I had no claim to it over you.
So I left it on the top shelf of that green-tiled kitchen,
where it shone in the cool half-light of dawn,
in the geranium-tinted afternoons,
in the soft sleepless hours like its own source of heat.
I do hope you are eating it now,
the slow dark honey of your disappointment,
rich with what had sustained us then,
all the sweeter and more nourishing
for eating alone.

# Temptation

I know it's blasphemous; years of Catholic school,
then Lutheran, were not for nothing.
But climbing to the monastery above
Jericho, the passage so narrow,
the cells so barren that we are tempted
to wonder

if it's a staged set for tourists to wonder
at, in our ignorance well-schooled
in pity, the poverty we make no attempt
to see beyond; we lean out over nothing
on the famous ledge, high and narrow
above

the cliffs, only the burnt-out sky above,
the trinket-sellers below. We wonder
at their excellent English, our narrow
escape from pleas to send their children to school,
to buy a necklace of stones, just one thing.
It is tempting

to imagine ourselves tempted,
here, with all we survey from above:
the crumbling town, the east bank, everything
in-between—the muddy line under-
mining what we're told is the Jordan, its cool
waters narrowed

to a trickle of salt. The question narrows
down to this: What was there to be tempted
by? The dry, gnarled orchards of bitter, cruel
fruit, plagued by bombs, checkpoints, and above
all, God? For us, to be torn asunder
means doing nothing.

Yet for those who live here, to do nothing
is not one of the options fast narrowing.
*Has there ever been peace here?* we wonder
aloud, as if any and all attempts
must fail as once before. To reach above
our schooling

in pessimism—nothing more foolish
but our narrow, unearned despair. Above
ourselves—a wonder not to be tempted.

## The Pursuit of Happiness

—As if happiness were something to be pursued,
hunted down like game or acquired, instead of
cultivated, sown even in poor, rocky soil,
not overly tended, allowed to grow a little wild.
Then again, it *was* the right to property they had in mind.

How you spent hours those early summer evenings
watering the planters out front, the hothouse hues
that hurt to look at, the lobelia's deepest blue,
the marigolds' blood-red and burnished gold,
the petunias' dazzling white heat.
You fastidiously pulled up anything faded or unsightly,
putting in what was already lovely, in blossom.
You worked at it: keeping up the neighborhood.

Certainly it was not too much to ask:
a well-kept flowerbox in the pursuit of happiness.

But it was in the north-facing back yard
behind the sagging fence that I scratched at
hard red clay, seeking my own:
the kind that's allowed to wilt from time to time
but comes in again hardier, the kind that thrives on
a little cutting back each spring.
The pungent, unruly mint and thyme,
misshapen squash that I'd hoped would nourish us:
indigenous, perennial, drought-resistant,
tough as weeds.

—Not to be confused with joy:
a completely different species of bloom,

like the first forsythia in still-wintering light,
blinding after weeks of waiting, or
the dogwood's pale abundance, expected yet
miraculous every time.

Elsewhere

Poems

Kyoko Uchida

# Four

Elsewhere

Poems

Kyoko Uchida

# After Weeks of Rain

After weeks of rain
the neighborhood children are trying out their lungs,
testing the green air at the highest registers,
the limits of their long-hushed breaths—
a piercing, urgent sunlight growing
hothouse-wild inside them.
Their howling stuns even the dogs into silence—
an unchoreographed Greek chorus calling out
unintelligible, fevered, ancient
in the raw and blinding light.

Then the quiet descending as suddenly as it was broken:
jagged, mean as barbed wire.
Bereft on my windowsill the Chinese moonflowers
bleach my room of evening.
Against a torn sky
the smallest sound rings metallic:
a warning.

# Domestication

I am domesticating my life.
I am learning to live in a small place
with walls newly painted white,
a mattress and a square kitchen table—
my singular needs and routines
simplified by the space I inhabit,

unlike in marriage:
a long uncharted trek through lushly shadowed gorges,
boarded-up neighborhoods, sandstone ruins,
wind-whipped fishing ports abandoned for the winter.
We picked our way down blind alleys and mud-deep trails,
and if we missed a turn, unable to read the signs,
we were taking in the scenery, getting to know the locals,
the children who gave directions in a language we didn't speak
as though it were the only one.
I thought we were mapping the world
out of the wilderness we shared.
I didn't see that you were scouting a sheltered clearing
deep in the forests of imported linens and furniture
where we would build a lovely house of many rooms—
while I fell behind, content to plot
the purple clover field humming with light
or pebbles underwater sharp as broken glass
or the jeweled heat of sun-split figs,
and never knew it was not enough.

Now, in this fourth-floor walk-up
without place settings or a sofa,
I am settling down to a quiet life indoors,
potted basil and rosemary in the window.
I am schooling myself to the slow harvest of hours,
the utter ease of feeding one's own narrow hunger.

## Tangential

1.
The day lengthens, turns interminable,
the light terminal, copper against windows on the river,
sharpening the hour to a point
fine enough to draw blood.
Wrought-iron shadows press their ends into
surfaces beaded with waiting,
with the dull heat of anticipation for
beginnings already beyond us.

2.
The fire escape cuts diagonally across my window
and its steep, heavy angle is the first thing I see
each day: its ascent against the eggshell lighting,
the geometry of morning.
Or perhaps of mourning.
I am told that I must grieve for all endings,
that they are each a kind of death.

3.
Or perhaps it is the geometry of gravity:
Learning to walk early, I'm told, I'd fallen down
the shag-carpeted stairs of our Houston townhouse
whenever my mother was out of sight.
I imagine my need to negotiate the space between *here* and
*there*, where my mother might be; the surprise each time of
the swiftness of it, the rush and whorl and scratch of
the few steps to the landing so fast I hardly feel it;
and that stunned moment just before I know
I've traveled the surest route to my mother's voice.

4.

Or perhaps the trigonometry of it:
We take as a sign what is merely symptom,
assume one angle to be right, when in fact
there are three sides:
opposite, adjacent, hypotenuse.
We co-sign agreements for reciprocal functions,
learn the inverse logic of our separate claims and grievances,
only to find ourselves
become tangential.

The equation does not always add up:
What is multiplied, what is squared
depend on the season's arc.
The angle of the fire escape is as narrow as
the vocabulary of our hearts and as weather-worn,
is as wide as the Earth's tilted axis,
off-center like the rest of us.

# In First Grade

Milk was 5¢ in the cafeteria.
Standing on tiptoe to peer over the plastic tray,
I learned to ask for what I wanted.
At home we were not asked; we always cleaned our plates.
But at school there were choices to be made every day:
Fried chicken or grilled cheese? Apple sauce or Jell-o?
It was as dizzying as a new box of crayons.
I chose to sit next to the skinny boy with freckles.
And when he scooted down the bench to sit with
the other boys, I was only just learning
this new language of longing.
I thought you had only to ask politely.
The next day he said, "*Please* don't sit next to me,"
and then I understood what it was
to inflict pain just by wanting, by wanting
something else.

# Hues

In the week I've sat at this window the treetops have turned
burnt pumpkin-gold and rust as brittle as early morning
light in mirrors, as hard and grainy as I imagine
the sugar in the leaves quickening to color—
the more sunlit the summer and the more sudden
the cold snap, the more brilliant the yellows and vermilions—
but this year the seasons have been slow in
changing, unraveling in fits and starts,
a false summer lingering on, unrelenting,
or perhaps too relenting, negotiating
an indifferent landscape.
Now what leaves are left dull to coppery ash, as though
the summer had not been sweet enough,
as though the end was too late in coming
to be beautiful.
Bare, the branches shadow to ink against evening,
deepening and deepening hues of dark descending,
breathtaking, familiar.